What A Way To Go

Todd McLeish

Verbis™
Publishing

For information contact

Verbis
Publishing
P.O. Box 2411
Hyannis, MA 02601

Verbis Publishing and the Verbis logo are trademarks of Verbis Publishing.

ISBN: 0-9648608-1-3

What A Way To Go

INTRODUCTION

Ordinarily, death is not a humorous subject.

We don't giggle during a funeral, laugh at the expense of someone on their deathbed, or make fun of a recently departed loved one. At least we shouldn't. Ann Landers, Dear Abby and Miss Manners have all said so.

But depersonalize it, give it a little time and there's no question about it, death, like life, can be incredibly bizarre.

It's common practice in modern Western society to joke about sex, religion, body parts and almost every bodily function imaginable. But until recently, death was a subject that remained taboo. No more!

Not only are the following strange-but-true death stories funny, but they also show how peculiar human society really is. For if not for the odd circumstances of our lives, we wouldn't be dying in the ludicrous ways described here.

If nothing else, this book is the ultimate demonstration that fact is stranger than fiction. Who could possibly have imagined a man having sex being crushed to death against the ceiling by a piano? Or that a man would die after falling into a coleslaw blender? Or how a flying canoe could kill a bicyclist?

Turn the pages and you'll find true stories about bizarre incidents of violence, like the anger counselor who beat his client to death, or the numerous cases of murder by bowling ball. You'll read about the nine people who died in three different manure pit accidents and the case of the giraffe-like okapi that died from listening to opera music. Then there's the unusual stories about funerals, wakes, cemeteries and morgues. The business side of dying can be just as freakish as the dying itself, sometimes even more so.

You might say that one would have to have the right kind of demented personality, outrageous sense of humor, or morbid curiosity to appreciate these stories, and you're right. But we all do.

Just think of the classic example: The accident on the highway. It's almost a cliché by now. You can't help but slow down and look. And aren't some of you disappointed when the ambulance has already driven away with the victims before you get close enough to see the results? Auto accidents make great stories at backyard barbecues or around the pinochle table. So do the stories in this book.

All of the stories in *What A Way To Go* are true accounts culled from daily newspapers. They aren't exaggerated stories or total fakes, like those found in the tabloids; they're real news stories reported by reputable journalists. The one thing all of the stories have in common is that they are truly weird.

While researching this book, I learned that morbid humor really seems to grow on you. When I first mentioned to friends and family about my idea of a book about unusual deaths, everyone thought I was sick. They were totally turned off, or most were. Ultimately, they were clipping articles, telling stories and jumping on the bandwagon. Even my mother-in-law, perhaps the most proper and self-conscious person I know, joined in, and when she even started laughing at some of the stories I unearthed, I knew I was on to something.

So, what are you waiting for? Turn the page and dig right in.

CRIME DOESN'T PAY

Newark, NJ -- A man stealing bricks was crushed to death when he removed the wrong brick and an abandoned building came tumbling down on top of him. "I told him it was dangerous to do that," said Hattie Mace, step-sister of Columbus Bridges.

Bridges had spent several years developing a network of buyers for bricks, which sell for 8 to 15 cents each. He was inside a three-story tenement owned by the Newark Housing Authority when the back half of the building collapsed.

Firefighters commandeered a forklift at a nearby construction site and used a giant crane to search for him.

* * *

Williamsport, Penn -- A would-be burglar froze to death after getting his bulky winter clothing stuck while climbing through a basement window.

When Henry Carlton's body was found, he was wedged halfway through a basement window, his legs inside and his head and arms outside.

* * *

Chicago -- After stealing a woman's purse in a high-crime area, 25 women and children chased down the thief and beat him to death with their fists.

"I heard one of the ladies say, 'You won't take nobody else's money no more'," said Dixie Hampton, a nearby resident who saw the beating.

* * *

St. Louis -- A drunken traveler was crushed to death in an airport trash compactor while hiding from authorities.

Joe Rutherford, 25, was traveling to Iowa with three companions, and drinking heavily, when he got into an unattended electric cart used by airport personnel and drove to the main terminal in a careless manner, scattering people on the concourse.

After airport workers began chasing him, Rutherford ran into a room and climbed into a trash chute leading to a dumpster. "He could have thought it was an air-conditioning chute and he could hide in there," said an airport worker. "But what he did not know is that there's an electric eye in the chute that activates the compactor in the dumpster."

* * *

Hamden, Conn. -- A shoplifter was killed when he slid off of a snow pile and under the wheels of a truck while fleeing from the store's security guard.

David Richardson, 39, of New Haven, stole a leather coat, a winter coat and a pair of pants from Steinbach's Department Store. When a store security guard chased him, Richardson ran onto a snow bank. The suspect then slid down the bank and under the back wheels of a 16-foot delivery truck.

* * *

New York -- A man was knocked down by a car, but was fortunately uninjured. When a bystander told him to pretend he was hurt to claim the insurance money, the man lay back down in the road.

Another car immediately drove by and crushed him to death.

* * *

Quick Takes

-- After leaving a restaurant without paying his $3.43 check, a Baltimore man took off running between two parked cars and was killed by a tractor trailer.

-- Police shot and killed a woman who was holding her cat at knifepoint in a grocery store in Oregon.

-- A burglar choked to death after a heavy patio door landed on his neck as he attempted to break into a lawyer's home.

-- A Tanzanian man convicted of stealing from a church, ran from court and jumped into a river. He was devoured by crocodiles.

MECHANICAL MONSTERS

Huntsville, Texas -- A bowling alley employee was killed when he became entangled in a pin-setting machine.

"It's unreal. It's one of those accidents that shouldn't have happened," said Richard Hartnett, Walker County justice-of-the-peace.

When Jimmie Carroll Ward II, 25, of Clute, tried to remove a bowling pin from the gutter underneath the pin-setter, the arms of the machine contracted when the resetting action was somehow triggered.

* * *

Scituate, RI -- An 18-year-old laundry worker died after being sucked into an industrial washing machine.

Steven Turcotte was loading a 10-foot-long washer when the machine apparently started up before the cover was in place.

***

Chicago -- An Army doctor has declared soda machines hazardous to your health.

Michael Cosio of the Walter Reed Army Medical Center in Washington documented 11 deaths from falling soda machines, including one victim who was found pinned to a wall with the soda machine resting on his neck. Others were crushed to death or asphyxiated.

"If you look at it from the victim's standpoint...if they get hurt if a machine lands on them, they have a 20 percent to 25 percent chance that they get killed," Cosio said. "Changes are needed to safeguard the public."

"The victims all were shaking or rocking the machines", he said, "some to shake loose a soda without paying, others because they're angry at the machine for keeping their money and not dispensing a soda."

"I usually just bang on the front or jiggle the coin return and if it doesn't work, I just walk away," Cosio said.

***

Selma, Ala. -- A large meat grinder started up unexpectedly, pulverizing a maintenance man who was working inside the machine.

"It was one of the most gruesome things I've ever seen in police work," police Lt. Robert Green said.

* * *

Boston -- A janitor at a Dorchester Laundromat was killed when he was trapped inside a dryer he was trying to clean.

The dryer apparently started automatically when a load of clothes was deposited inside by a conveyor belt. Police said that another employee reported hearing a thumping noise from inside the machine, but did not know what was causing it.

The dryer discharged the man onto a conveyor belt when it finished its cycle.

* * *

Indianapolis -- A woman scavenging for aluminum cans in a dumpster was crushed to death after the container was hauled away by a garbage truck and its contents compacted.

Leona Troutman, 34, was seen climbing into the trash bin by a couple staying at a nearby motel. They tried to warn the driver but were unable to get his attention before he drove off. The bin's contents were compacted on the way to the city's trash incinerator.

* * *

Tokyo -- A Japanese government official reported that robots have killed ten Japanese men. The official said six people died when industrial robots made unexpected movements , such as turning left instead of right, and crushed workers. One worker, trying to repair a robot's arm, was killed when the arm shot upward and struck him. At least five or six injuries involving robots are reported each year.

* * *

Quick Takes

-- A Baltimore man died when he fell in a blender used to mix coleslaw. He was loading the ingredients at the time.

-- A food service worker in California was accidentally killed in a 5-foot deep mixing bowl. He was cleaning the inside of the bowl when another employee turned on the beater.

ALL IN A DAY'S WORK

Albany, NY -- A Salvation Army employee working a warehouse was crushed to death by a 1,200 pound bundle of used clothing.

Michael Raughter, 57, was found under a rectangular bundle of clothing measuring about 8 feet by 5 feet. He was a graduate of the Salvation Army's drug and alcohol rehabilitation program and had lived at the facility for six years.

* * *

Detroit -- A dairy farm worker in Menominee, Mich., was overcome by methane fumes and died when he slipped into a manure pit, and four others died trying to rescue him. "It appeared they were cleaning it and the first victim just happened to slip," said Dr. Paul Haupt, county medical examiner. "One man accidentally slipped down the inclined plane; a second went down in and was overcome also. Then another went down to get the other two, and so on and so on."

Five men died in the mishap. Four other men died in similar circumstances in Minnesota.

* * *

Honolulu -- An anger-management counselor lost his temper and punched a man who arrived at his class drunk. The man lapsed into a coma and died.

Thirty-two-year-old Miguel Gonzales was ordered by Family Court to attend the anger-management class after he had been arrested for beating his girlfriend. The counselor, Charles Mahuka, was on parole for attempted murder.

* * *

Junction City, Ore. -- A farm worker suffocated to death when tons of grass seed buried him in a 20-foot-high storage bin.

Dennis Thomas, 22, of Eugene, jumped into the bin to help the seed drain. But the seed caved in around him and fellow farm employees and rescue workers were not able to dig Thomas out before he suffocated.

* * *

Stockholm -- In an effort to stop a fight, a 286-pound bouncer killed a restaurant guest by sitting on him.

The bouncer grabbed an unruly 26-year-old man by the head and held him to the ground by sitting on him. When bystanders noticed that the man was having trouble breathing, they tried to get the bouncer to stop, but he refused because he thought the man was bluffing.

* * *

Huntsville, Texas -- As editor of the Texas Death Row Journal, it's Jim Beathard's duty to say something nice about people not especially known for their kindness.

A convicted killer himself, Beathard writes obituaries about his recently departed neighbors on death row. He gets more practice than he'd like in the nation's most active death penalty state.

* * *

Ceres, Calif. -- Three janitors trying to freeze a gopher to death caused an explosion that injured 19 people at an elementary school, most of them students.

The Fowler Elementary School janitors were blown out of a utility room when one of them tried to light a cigarette after spraying the rodent with a freezing solvent used to clean gum and wax off floors.

Two janitors were hospitalized. Sixteen pupils were treated for minor injuries. The gopher survived and was later released in a field.

* * *

Volant, Penn. -- A 300-pound man fell into a sandwashing machine and suffocated under several tons of sand after a plank broke beneath him.

"Tuffy" Reeher, 32, stepped onto the plank while trying to figure out why the machine had stalled. The wood snapped under his weight, and he fell ten feet into the machine.

Before rescuers could reach him, the machine suddenly restarted and sucked him under.

* * *

Paris -- Firemen tackling a forest fire in the south of France called in a special flying boat that sucked up water from the Mediterranean and dropped it onto the blazing trees.

The next day, while sifting through the embers, rescuers found the body of a man who had been killed by falling from a great height He was wearing a bathing suit, snorkel and swim fins.

* * *

Quick Takes

-- A security equipment company owner died as he tried to show that knives can't puncture bulletproof vests. The vest stopped the knife the first time, but the second attempt killed him.

-- A Colorado man accidentally fell into a brickmaking machine and was mixed in a batch of bricks. The bricks were later buried at a local cemetery.

-- A 23-year-old candy factor worker in France was crushed to death when 5,000 pounds of marshmallows fell on him.

-- An Israeli soldier on leave from combat duty met his end at a pizza parlor when he was sucked into a giant dough mixer and kneaded to death.

-- After singing the line "You can only live so long," an opera singer suffered a heart attack and fell 10 feet from a ladder during a performance.

SELF-DESTRUCTION

Abidjan, Ivory Coast -- A man upset with the death of his country's president jumped into the ruler's palace moat where he was eaten by crocodiles.

The unidentified young man told onlookers that he could no longer bear to live without President Felix Houphouet-Boigny, who ruled the Ivory Coast for 33 years until his death.

"If Houphouet is dead, I don't see why I should go on living," the man said shortly before jumping in the moat.

* * *

Bartow, FL -- Distraught that his girlfriend was getting back together with her husband, Edward Leonard Hand pointed a gun to his chin and tried to kill himself.

He killed the husband instead.

The bullet passed through Hand's chin, out his right cheek and struck and killed Ronald Gauley.

Hand, 33, was hospitalized for three weeks. He was then charged with manslaughter, third-degree murder, shooting a firearm in an occupied dwelling and two counts each of armed kidnapping and aggravated assault.

* * *

Los Angeles -- In a particularly unusual suicide, death-row inmate William Kogut blew himself up with a pipe bomb made of playing cards.

Kogut scraped the red spots off a deck of cards and filled a hollow bed leg with the dots, thereby creating a destructive weapon. He then placed the bomb on his cell's heater and put his head on the bomb. The heat detonated the bomb.

* * *

Pittsburgh -- Apparently distraught that her ex-husband was going to the Super Bowl without her, the former wife of San Diego Chargers quarterbacks coach Dwain Painter killed herself hours after the AFC championship game.

* * *

San Diego -- The death of Ronald Opus caused serious headaches for the San Diego coroner's office. When the medical examiner viewed Opus' body, he concluded that Opus died from a shotgun wound to the head. The decedent had jumped from the top of a ten-story building intending to commit suicide. (He left a note indicating his despondency.)

As he fell past the ninth floor, he was instantly killed by a shotgun blast through a window. "Neither the shooter nor the decedent was aware that a safety net had been erected at the eighth floor level to protect some window washers and that Opus, therefore, would not have been able to complete his suicide," said medical examiner Stuart Mills.

The fact that Opus' suicidal intent would not have been successful caused the medical examiner to feel that he had a homicide on his hands.

The room on the ninth floor whence the shotgun blast emanated was occupied by an elderly man and his wife. They were arguing and he was threatening her with the shotgun. He was so upset that when he pulled the trigger, he completely missed his wife and the pellets went through the window striking Opus.

"When one intends to kill subject A," explained Mills, "but kills subject B in the attempt, one is guilty of the murder of subject B."

When confronted with this charge, the old man and his wife were both adamant that neither knew that the shotgun was loaded. The old man said it was his long-standing habit to threaten his wife with the unloaded shotgun.

He had no intention to murder her, therefore, the killing of Opus appeared to be an accident. That is, the gun had been accidentally loaded.

The continuing investigation turned up a witness who saw the old couple's son loading the shotgun approximately six weeks prior to the fatal incident. It transpired that the old lady had cut off her son's financial support and the son, knowing the propensity of his father to use the shotgun threateningly, loaded the gun with the expectation that his father would shoot the mother. The case now becomes one of murder on the part of the son for the death of Ronald Opus.

But there was an exquisite twist. Further investigation revealed that the son (Ronald Opus) had become increasingly despondent over the failure of his attempt to engineer his mother's murder. This led him to jump off the ten-story building, only to be killed by a shotgun blast, through a ninth story window.

The medical examiner closed the case as a suicide.

* * *

Quick Takes

-- Distraught over learning her husband had been unfaithful, a woman in Prague jumped from a third-story window. She landed on her husband as he entered the building. She survived and he didn't.

-- The cancellation of the TV series Battlestar Galactica prompted a teenager to jump to his death off a bridge.

-- A man committed suicide when he learned that his mother-in-law had tricked him into marrying the uglier of her two daughters.

-- A pregnant woman hung herself in London because of delays in construction of her new baby's bathroom.

-- An accused murderer killed himself while being held at a psychiatric institute by driving two ball-point pens through his heart.

-- A Seoul housewife killed herself over her failure to prepare her husband's lunch in time for his company picnic.

-- An Illinois man killed himself over an argument about drapes by cutting a hole in his waterbed and drowning himself.

-- A retired Sri Lankan police driver hung himself because his wife didn't cook him fish for lunch.

-- Armando Cassa was so depressed when he was reported to have died in a fire that he jumped to his death from a high-rise building.

-- When a crowd of 50 people gathered on a bridge to watch as a girl attempted suicide, the bridge collapsed under their weight and killed nine of them. The girl survived.

ROAD KILL

Plymouth, Mass. -- A canoe which flew off the back of a speeding pickup truck killed a 63-year-old bicyclist who was riding in a line with 20 others.

"We're always wearing helmets, but there are certain situations a helmet can't protect you from," said the man's daughter.

* * *

Cold Spring, Ky. -- A coffin killed the driver of a hearse when a head-on collision caused the coffin to crush the main against the dashboard.

As Jack Volkering, 59, was returning from a funeral, a car struck the hearse causing the coffin to break through a metal holding post. The coffin then struck Volkering in the back as the dashboard and steering wheel hit him in the chest.

Another hearse picked up the body in the coffin immediately after the accident and it was buried as scheduled.

* * *

Port Chester, NY -- A truck carrying caskets and another one carrying tombstones were involved in a fatal accident on Interstate 95.

Three northbound tractor-trailers were involved in the accident. One had broken down; a second driver stopped to help; and a third plowed into the others.

The driver of the casket truck, Paul Hebert, was killed when he was pinned between his broken-down truck and another truck whose driver had stopped to help him. The driver who rammed them was carrying granite tombstones.

* * *

Abilene, Kan. -- A man was killed after falling from the back of a pickup and then run over again and again by passing cars. His companions, meanwhile, drove 40 miles before noticing he was missing.

Hubbard White, 61, was killed instantly when he was run over by the first vehicle, a horse trailer.

* * *

Sacramento -- Congressman Vic Fazio is telling anyone who cares to listen that he isn't dead, no matter how many sympathy cards and floral arrangements come into his office.

The cards and flowers for the West Sacramento Democrat started after state Assemblyman Tom Hannigan introduced a bill to name a portion of a highway near Woodland the Vic Fazio Freeway. Such honors are usually reserved for the dead.

* * *

Kalamazoo, Mich. -- James Burns knew his dump truck needed repairs, but he couldn't find the source of the problem.

So he got a friend to drive the truck on a highway while Burns hung underneath so he could ascertain the source of the troubling noise.

Burns' clothes got caught on something, and his friend later found him wrapped in the drive shaft.

* * *

Phoenix -- When the Arizona Highway Patrol found a pile of smoldering metal embedded into the side of a cliff near a curve in the road, they thought it was the site of an airplane crash. But it was a car.

Apparently the man obtained a Jet Assisted Take Off (JATO) unit used to give heavy military transport planes an extra push for taking off from short airfields. The man then drove his Chevy Impala into the desert and found a long straight stretch of road.

He then attached the JATO unit to his car, jumped in and fired off the JATO.

As best as could be determined, the man was driving somewhere between 250 and 300 miles per hour when he came to the curve. The brakes were completely burned away from trying to slow down.

* * *

Quick Takes

-- A motorcycle rider died when his ball-point pen punctured his body during a minor traffic accident.

-- A Japanese man choked to death when he became entangled in his seat-belt on the first day of the country's mandatory seat-belt law.

-- A motorist who ran over a porcupine decided to put the animal out of its misery by clubbing it with a shotgun. The gun went off killing the motorist.

BLOOPERS AND BONERS

Margate, NJ -- A pallbearer was crushed to death by the coffin containing world-record hot-dog eater Hubert Ross.

During a rainy graveside service, the pallbearer slipped and fell into the grave. The coffin then fell in and killed him.

* * *

Cologne, Germany -- A passionate lover's embrace ended in tragedy when the couple lost their balance and fell from a balcony onto a concrete floor. A 25-year-old woman died and her 24-year-old boyfriend sustained serious injuries.

They fell together about 13 feet outside a building where they had gone to a party.

* * *

Laguna Hills, Calif. -- A Brinks guard suffered a fatal heart attack after $13,000 worth of quarters, weighing 1-1/4 tons, fell on him inside an armored car when the driver braked to avoid another vehicle.

According to the California Highway Patrol, guard Hrand Arkilian, 34, was not seated in the chair guards are suppose to use when the vehicle is in motion.

* * *

Quick Takes

-- New Zealand daredevil Bobby Leach, who survived two trips over Niagara Falls in a barrel, died after slipping on an orange peal.

-- Veteran mountaineer Gerard Hommel, who climbed Mount Everest six times, fell off a ladder while changing a light bulb and died.

-- While praying in thanks for his daughter's escape from a car accident, a man was killed by a falling bag of cement.

-- A South Carolina prison inmate electrocuted himself as he tried to fix his radio earphones while sitting on a steel toilet.

-- While being baptized, a Massachusetts man slipped into deep water and drowned.

-- When two men tried to repossess her washing machine, a Texas woman started shooting at them. One bullet ricocheted off the machine and killed her nephew.

-- A man won an argument with another man over who would sit on the only chair in the shade of a tree, then died when the tree fell on him.

-- As he was congratulating himself for finding a lucky four-leaf clover, a man slipped on some wet grass and fell off a cliff, plunging 150 feet to his death.

-- A Philippine treasure hunter was killed while trying to saw open a World War II bomb he found. It exploded.

THE LIVING DEAD

Springfield, Ohio -- An 87-year-old woman woke up while being embalmed despite showing no signs of life before being taken to a funeral home.

"The lady died away for a while and later came back to," said the funeral director Robbie Caldwell. "The lady was laying there. She had no pulse, no blood pressure, nothing. She was just gone."

Ms. Caldwell refused to answer additional questions.

* * *

Artesia, NM -- After Mary Bratcher ran over and killed her dog, the family buried Brownie in a field.

The next day, a dirt-covered Brownie was on the porch.

"He was real cold, and he wasn't breathing real good," said Mrs. Bratcher. "It freaked me out big time."

The mongrel mutt lost an eye and broke his right shoulder in the accident. But he was no ghost, says veterinarian Bill Livingston. "He was probably in a coma."

The dog has responded well to treatment and now has a new name: Lazarus, after the biblical figure who was raised from the dead.

* * *

Knoxville, Tenn. -- Funeral arrangements were being made for a retired coal minor when the man started breathing again.

"The family of course thinks it's a miracle," said a hospital spokeswoman. "They've really been on a roller coaster."

Hospital personnel declared S. Thomas Barnett, 71, dead. Papers were signed to transport the body to the morgue and funeral arrangements were made. Then, as a nurse started to remove his belongings from a closet, she heard him breathing.

Dr. Gene Aaby, a cardiac surgeon at the hospital, speculated that Barnett lived through the event because he has black lung disease. "It's just a theory," he said. "Because he has black lung disease, his brain has learned to function with less oxygen."

* * *

Albany, NY -- An 86-year-old woman spent nearly 90 minutes in a hospital morgue refrigerator after a coroner mistakenly pronounced her dead.

Mildred Clark was found unconscious in her apartment, declared dead by the county coroner, and taken to the morgue at Albany Medical Center Hospital.

The morgue supervisor preparing to transfer Clark's body to a funeral home heard breathing coming from the body bag, unzipped it and found Clark was alive.

* * *

St. Petersburg, FL -- A 75-year-old woman who was declared dead and wrapped in a plastic shroud was found gasping by her children after they rushed to the hospital.

Doctors at Palms of Pasadena Hospital had tried to revive Emma Brady, but pronounced her dead of cardiac arrest.

* * *

Quick Takes

-- A London woman was declared dead by a doctor after a suicide attempt, but an undertaker heard her snoring in the hospital morgue.

-- When Antonio Percelli, mistakenly declared dead, climbed out of his casket during his funeral, his mother immediately died of a heart attack.

PERISHABLE PETS

Auburn, NH -- A State Police dog that killed two sheep and a pet goat was fired from the force and the State Police were required to reimburse the owner of the animals.

Mark Sanford and his 10-year-old son watched as the Rottweiler, Sirius, killed his animals. The dog had escaped from his pen at Trooper Patrick Palmer's home.

* * *

Port Huron, Mich. -- A cat owner whose pet was bashed to death by his friends says he may have inadvertently spurred the attack when he shouted the animal's name, Killer.

"One guy was petting the cat and it scratched him. The cat was thrown and it stunned the cat" he said. "I called out her name, 'Killer!' I don't think they understood what I said."

* * *

Pensacola, FL -- Rufus Godwin learned the fate of his missing hunting dog Flojo when a 500-pound alligator coughed up the animal's electronic tracking collar.

Then, when trappers slit open the gator's belly, they found the tags and collars of six more hunting hounds.

For the past 20 years, hunting dogs have been disappearing in the Blackwater River State Forest. Their owners, members of the Blackwater River and Santa Rosa Fox Hunting Associations, thought people were stealing them. The thief, it turns out, was the gator, which had turned a game trail into his private diner, grabbing dogs as they ran across Coldwater Creek in pursuit of game. Their barking apparently was his dinner bell.

* * *

Madison, Wis. -- Boogs the cat had faced execution as a dangerous animal after growling at neighbors, eating a neighbor cat's food and nipping an animal control officer who picked him up. He had also menaced and bit other people.

But a state judge lifted the death sentence, instead ordering the cat's owner to keep the cat on a leash and muzzled. The reprieve came after a letter-writing campaign.

* * *

Cairo -- Six people drowned while trying to rescue a chicken that had fallen into a well. The chicken survived. An 18-year-old farmer was the first to descend into the 60-foot well. He drowned after an undercurrent of water pulled him down.

His sister and two brothers, none of whom could swim well, went in one-by-one to help him, but also drowned. The elderly farmers then came to help, but they drowned too.

* * *

Harahan, LA -- A snake collector was strangled to death in his home by his 200 pound pet python, despite stabbing it several times with a knife.

His body was found after he failed to show up for work. It took three people to force the 16-foot python, named Ebenezer, into an animal shelter truck.

* * *

Tangent, Oregon -- She was, perhaps, the fattest cat in Oregon, in terms of her inheritance, that is. Now Kitty Cat, the 19-year-old feline who inherited her owner's $250,000 estate in 1983, has died.

The City of Tangent is the new heir.

Kitty Cat's remains were cremated. A cat-sized wooden casket was made in 1990, and Kitty Cat has long had a marble tombstone that reads "Kitty Cat: A True Friend."

The city will gain ownership of the 1916 five-bedroom farmhouse, once owned by Kitty Cat's owner, John Bass.

METEOROLOGICAL MORTALITY

London -- 62-year-old Iris Somerville was killed when lightning struck the metal underweaving of her brassiere as she walked through a London park.

A coroner concluded that a burn mark on her chest matched the pattern of metal reinforcing her bra.

* * *

Bossier City, LA -- A man standing in the stern of his new boat raised his hands, looked skyward and declared "Here I am," just before a lightning bolt struck him dead.

Graves Thomas, a 40-year-old Shreveport attorney, died of electrocution. There was no thunder, lightning or sign of lightning before the killer bolt struck.

* * *

Los Angeles -- A 488-pound yellow umbrella stuck in the ground by the artist Christo, was uprooted by a gust of wind and crushed a passer-by.

The umbrella was one of 1,760 giant umbrellas Christo had placed in Tejon Pass, in the mountains north of Los Angeles. Another 1,340 blue umbrellas were raised in Japan.

* * *

Hardin, M0 -- Sheriff's deputies and National Guardsmen fought through floodwaters in an attempt to retrieve caskets and vaults dislodged from a rural cemetery and washed downstream by the Missouri River.

"I was out there 'til about noon today and they're still rounding them up," said the County Sheriff. "I've seen 25 or 30 that were lodged against some trees and the current was so strong, we couldn't get them out."

Nearly 100 coffins or vaults had been recovered, some of them open.

* * *

Orange, VA -- A bolt of lightning in the night killed 30 pedigreed black Angus cattle huddling in the rain.

George Ahlfield said he heard the loud crack of thunder, but wasn't prepared for the grisly scene. Heaps of dead cows lay scattered in the field, with the surviving animals hovering nearby. The thunderstorm killed about half his herd.

* * *

Sneads, FL -- Nearly a quarter-of-a-million bats drowned when Tropical Storm Alberto flooded their cave.

A wildlife biologist said he saw big piles of bat skeletons in a "maternity cave" where an estimated 85,000 adult female bats and 160,000 of their young had roosted before the nearby Apalachicola River overflowed.

"The ceiling was still dotted with bat carcasses," Jeff Gore of the Florida Game & Fresh Water Fish Commission, said.

MANIACAL MOTIVES

Hong Kong -- A Taiwanese woman killed her mother-in-law and stabbed her mother because she thought her own beauty made the other women expendable.

Hu Pao-yin, 35, told a district court she knifed her mother-in-law on Christmas Eve "because I am the most beautiful woman in the world and the existence of other women is unnecessary."

A day earlier, Hu had stabbed her adoptive mother in the back. She survived.

* * *

Rome -- A 21-year-old butcher stabbed his future father-in-law to death after an argument about when to remove pasta from boiling water.

Sergio Noir was asked to leave the table during lunch after telling his fiancée's mother she ruined a pasta dish by letting it boil too long. Things escalated from there. The father then slapped his daughter, Noir's fiancée, and refused to let her leave the house with Noir. At that point the enraged young man stabbed the father to death.

* * *

St. Louis -- A man upset because his younger brother had used six rolls of toilet paper in two days shot and killed him.

Nathan Hicks, 35, confessed that the shooting stemmed from an argument over toilet paper. Hicks told officers he had bought an eight-roll package of toilet paper and became enraged because Herbert had used up six of the rolls in two days.

* * *

Columbiana, Ala. -- A university debate coach was sentenced to life in prison for stabbing his star student to death.

Prosecutors claimed William Slagle, a debate coach at Samford University, killed Rex Bartley Copeland because the student had failed to adequately prepare for a competition.

* * *

Brooklyn Center, Minn. -- A man died after he was beat up by fellow bowlers in a midnight dispute over lane courtesy and a bowling ball.

Mark Robert Bullard, 28, was hit several times and fell possibly striking his head on a table at Earl Brown Bowl. An autopsy said Bullard died of blunt force injury.

* * *

Cleveland -- A landlord murdered a tenant who dropped her pants and mooned him during an argument.

Police said tenant Shirley McCool dropped her pants and mooned her landlord, Edward Drewery, when he threatened to evict her friend. McCool, who was standing in the street, was shot once in the head.

* * *

New Delhi, India -- Four college freshmen were killed by police who tried to stop them from cheating on exams.

The melee occurred in the town of Salsingsarai after the students opened their books and notes during final exams. The students threw explosives at a government jeep and tried to set fire to the railway station. Police opened fire, killing four of them.

The annual standardized test is the main criteria for a passing grade, but students aren't suppose to use their books. Students maintained they needed their notes, however, because they have been so poorly taught.

* * *

Birmingham, Ala. -- A foot race that began as a challenge during a wedding reception ended with the loser shooting the winner to death outside a church.

Witnesses said Harry Mason and James Mays agreed to the race, with $20 going to the victor. Both had attended a reception for Princess and Melin Coleman, married earlier at the city's botanical gardens.

Mason, who was wearing wedding attire and dress shoes, beat Mays, who was wearing tennis shoes. Moments later, Mason was shot in the head.

* * *

New York -- The referee of a basketball game sponsored by drug dealers in a city park was beaten to death over a bad call. The victim, an elementary school gym teacher, apparently didn't realize who sponsored the game.

Police sources said that the Supreme Team, a crack gang that controls the Baisley Park housing project in Queens, got the game up as a "public service." The referee, Greg Vaughn, 33, was killed in a park near the project when a player, apparently angry about a call, struck him over the head.

* * *

Manila -- A man stabbed and killed his brother and wounded a friend when they failed to agree that former first lady Imelda R. Marcos is prettier than the Princess of Wales.

Gerardo and Felino Delmo were drinking beer with their friend Manuel Dacaney at their home in suburban Manila when they began discussing the relative beauty of the two women. When Gerardo Delmo, 29, said Marcos is prettier, his brother and Decanay disagreed.

"Don't belittle Meldy, she's still the most beautiful woman in the world," Gerardo Delmo said before he allegedly ran to the kitchen to grab a knife.

* * *

Alton, Ill. -- Dorothea and Mary Margaret Beck lived in the same house together all their 68 years. The twin sisters worked at the same hospital. They walked their poodle and shopped for groceries together.

But one day Dorothea Beck beat and kicked her sister to death after she refused to eat.

Neighbors said the fraternal twins had spent their lives together, never marrying or moving away from home. But Eddie Holmes, who had known the sisters since 1967, said they had very different personalities.

"The little one, who died, she seemed like the humble one," he said. "The big one would raise hell all the time. Some days she would fuss and cuss and carry on all day."

* * *

New York -- A Brooklyn woman met her husband at the door with a shotgun blast because he went fishing, leaving her home alone to recover from hemorrhoid surgery.

After seeing her husband traipse off with a cooler of beer to spend the day with his friends, Gail Murphy was furious. When she heard him return, she walked to the porch with a shotgun and fired through the door.

* * *

Quick Takes

-- One teenage boy killed another because the first claimed he looked better in women's clothing than did the other's girlfriend.

-- A man who complained to his son that the volume on the television was too loud, shot the teenager in the head.

-- A woman was killed by her husband for overcooking a meal. Seventeen years earlier, the man killed his first wife for undercooking a meal.

-- Two soccer players were shot to death by fans in Uruguay in order to prevent a goal from being scored.

-- A cook at a Whataburger franchise in Forth Worth killed a customer who was upset that the restaurant had run out of large hamburger buns.

-- A woman murdered her sister because she cooked too many potatoes for dinner.

-- In Manila, two men killed in an argument over which came first, the chicken or the egg.

-- In Chicago, a man was arrested for beating his stepson to death because, when reciting the alphabet, the child couldn't get past "G".

-- A teenager died after he was shot while a friend fought with another boy over a 15-cent cherry Popsicle.

-- A man who lost an early-morning Bible-quoting contest murdered the man who beat him.

-- A Long Island man was stabbed to death for chastising his killer for not washing his hands after using the bathroom.

-- A business executive strangled his wife to death after an argument about where on the table to place the mustard.

-- A Louisiana man was shot dead during an argument over the proper way to season a roast turkey.

GOING IN STYLE

Pittsburg, PA -- Dying of complications from intestinal surgery, fireworks handler Brian Kelly of Detroit told his family, "I just want to be a big firecracker."

So his ashes were rolled into a 12-inch shell that exploded into red and green stars during the grand finale of the Pyrotechnics Guild International convention in Pittsburgh.

* * *

Orlando, FL -- The miles Louise Tanner walked were for a camel, a 2,300 pound dromedary by the name of Gus that she raised from a calf in the front yard of her home here.

So the sight of Gus, draped in black and followed by pallbearers, brought tearful smiles from those who came to Woodlawn Memorial Park to bury the 75-year-old widow.

"It was really touching and sweet," Margaret Stephenson said of Gus' presence at the graveside service for her sister. "We all cracked up with tears."

* * *

Rockford, Ill. -- Ever had a twinge of curiosity about what your wake will be like? Irene Lathom has been to hers and she had a great time.

Lathom, 72, invited nearly 200 relatives and friends to a "B.C." or "before cremation" party. The soiree was billed on a flier as the "premiere show before the grand finale."

Most of the "mourners" agreed that the guest of honor who married four times and is known to wear a Bo Derek wig from time-to-time, is one of a kind.

* * *

New York -- You see them dressed to the nines for award ceremonies, or in costume on stage. But what would they like to wear for their final appearance, before the coffin is closed?

"The dress Jack Lemmon wore in 'Some Like It Hot,' " was rocker Alice Cooper's pick for eternal-wear.

"A rented tuxedo," syndicated columnist Dave Barry said.

"The only thing I'd want to be caught dead in is my wedding ring. You don't need clothes where you're going." Grateful Dead drummer Mickey Hart said.

* * *

Alameda, CA -- As a minister, Al Carpenter wanted to save people's souls. As a mortician, he wants to save them money. Carpenter provides blueprints for build-it-yourself coffins for customers willing to supply the wood and the work.

The plan costs $9.95 and materials would run about $70, Carpenter said, compared with factory-made caskets that can cost thousands of dollars.

But economy isn't the only benefit. There's the "positive experience" of building a loved one's final resting place, he said.

* * *

Indianapolis -- Mourners wanting to get their loved ones to the cemetery in comfort may want to consider the latest in funeral coaches; one with velvet seats and options like a stereo, refrigerator and microwave oven.

The Airstream Family Funeral Coach gets 9 to 12 miles per gallon and eliminates traffic snarls resulting from caravans of mourners traveling to the cemetery.

All this comfort and practicality doesn't come cheap, however. Funeral home directors can expect to pay $52,000 to $73,000 for the aluminum coaches.

The 28-foot vehicle constructed from a motor home chassis can carry 16 people up front and the dear departed in a separate compartment towards the rear. The casket can be surrounded by shelves of flowers and be bathed in spotlight.

"Some of the relatives may not have seen each other for 20 years," said Karl H. Croel, salesman for the Ohio-based Airstream. "The time that they get a chance to talk together is when they're together in the privacy of this coach."

"I think it's a little much," said Christina Burkholder, who works at her family's funeral home in Seymour.

She said a hearse or a limousine commands respect. But if onlookers saw the Airstream coach cruising down the street: "You'd think it was the Brady Bunch going to the Grand Canyon."

* * *

Exeter, England -- Teddy Corbett-Winder has organized his own funeral to avoid bothering anyone with a mortician's bill.

The 72-year-old retired businessman is ready to meet his maker for a bargain price of less than $180. A carpenter made a chipboard box coffin for less than $125, and a friend will take him to his final resting place in a station wagon.

Corbett-Winder keeps dirty laundry in the coffin under his bed at his home in Exeter, southwest England, until it is needed. "All they will have to do is roll me out of my bed and straight into the box," he said.

He has also written his epitaph: "Edmund Frederick Corbett-Winder, 1916-? No Rip Off."

He has already had a trial run for his cremation. "It was beautiful, but a bit hard on the backside. I'll have to put in a cushion and pillow," he said.

* * *

Milwaukee -- Planning on dying someday? Need a coffee table in the meantime? Or a bookcase or chest?

You're in luck. Two entrepreneurs in River Falls, Wis. have come up with a functional invention that is, quite literally, to die for. It's a multi-purpose, mail-order, make-it-yourself combination coffee table and coffin kit.

Fred and Mary Lehmann have received dozens of inquiries on the $989 item and been interviewed by everyone from Paul Harvey to the BBC. They haven't sold one yet.

The ads the Lehmanns run read, "For those who wish to participate in saying good-bye more simply."

And we're talking simple. The kit contains six pre-cut panels of solid willow wood, 50 screws, six black painted steel handles, sandpaper and assembly instructions; it takes a couple of hours at the most to put it together.

RECREATIONAL EXPIRATIONS

Moscow -- A rare electrical imbalance in the brain caused the death of a chess player whose head exploded in the middle of a championship match. No one else was hurt in the explosion, but four players and three officials at the Moscow Candidate Masters' Chess Championships were sprayed with blood and brain

matter when Nikolai Titov's head exploded. Doctors say he suffered from a condition called hyper-cerebral electrosis.

He was deep in concentration with his eyes focused on the board," says Titov's opponent, Vladimir Dobrynin. "All of a sudden his hands flew to his temples and he screamed in pain. Then, as If someone had put a bomb in his cranium, his head popped like a firecracker."

* * *

New Delhi -- In India, war games with kites are popular. Enthusiasts often put a paste of boiled rice mixed with glass dust on the string to increase the sharpness and cut the thread of other kites.

But in a freak accident, the sharp line of one kite was blamed for slashing the throat of a passing motorcyclist.

* * *

New York -- "We've had some bizarre occurrences before," said Suffolk County detective Kevin Cronin. "But I've never heard of anyone being killed by a keg."

But that's exactly what happened when a beer keg exploded after being placed into a bonfire during a party. The victim, Chester Vesloski was standing 40 feet from the fire when the keg blew up.

The keg was later found 250 feet away.

* * *

Bocholt, Germany -- A band musician died of a brain injury when the trombonist behind him jerked the slide of his instrument forward and struck him in the back of the head.

The incident prompted the band director to call for jazz music to be outlawed in Germany.

Trombonist Peter Neimeyer got carried away as the Gratzfield College band played "When the Saints Go Marching In." As he moved with the beat, he jerked forward causing the round metal slide on his instrument to hit trumpet player Dolph Mohr, killing him instantly.

"The slide struck him in the worst possible place, the vulnerable spot just behind and below the left ear," said the medical examiner. "This caused the bone fragments to pierce his brain."

The incident caused a storm of controversy over whether or not American jazz should be played in German colleges.

"I believe the music is to blame," said band director Heinrich Sommer. "I've always said jazz is dangerous music."

"Our musicians can't control themselves when they play it. They move and rock back and forth, creating chaos. If I had my way, jazz would be outlawed in Germany. I've been directing bands for 30 years and I've never heard of anyone dying while playing a German march."

* * *

Chicago -- During a party on the thirty-ninth floor of Chicago's Prudential Building, lawyer Reginald Tucker, 29, accidentally ran out a window and plunged to his death.

In the middle of the party, Tucker took off his glasses and started racing a co-worker. He apparently didn't see the window at the end of one corridor.

As he continued running, Tucker crashed through the window and fell to his death.

* * *

Arvada, Colo. -- A bungee company crew member was killed when he jumped from a hot-air balloon and hit the ground before the cord could snap him skyward.

William Brotherton, 20, was testing the equipment when he took the first, and last, jump of the day.

Obviously, either the balloon, which was tethered to the ground, was not high enough or the bungee cord was too long.

* * *

Aubenas, Frances -- Circus archer, Tony Bertolazzi, was trying to burst a small balloon held by a partner about 30 feet away during a performance of the Christiane Gruss Circus. But he missed.

Instead, the arrow flew past a protective shield set up behind the target and into the orchestra area. It struck a trumpet player in the face and killed him.

* * *

Peking -- The Chinese government is going to build a multi-million dollar golf course and an amusement park where 13 Ming Dynasty emperors are buried,and the decision has provoked a storm of protests.

In ceremonies marked by fireworks, a drum-and-cymbal band and a five-yard drive off the tee, Chinese and Japanese officials broke ground for the $10.7 million 18-hole course.

The festivities featured a top Communist Party official taking his first uncertain swipe at a golf ball. Politburo member Wang Zhen used a club gripper better suited for a hoe to drive a ball five yards as 100 spectators watched.

The course will be built on a field painted light green, dark green and brown for the ceremonies to show what the links will look like near 13 tombs of Ming Dynasty (1368-1644) emperors. And that has sparked some controversy.

* * *

Koblenz, Germany -- Two Boy Scouts died after a rope snapped during a giant tug-of-war by 650 people who were trying to win a place in the Guinness Book of Records.

The thumb-thick nylon rope broke and whipped back during the contest on Sunday, hitting a 9-year-old boy so hard he died.

A ten-year-old boy and at least 24 others were injured, five seriously, by being crushed or hitting the ground hard as the tension on the rope broke.

* * *

New Haven, CT -- It was never intended for this purpose, of course. But in the short, fast life of William Villanueva, smoking "ill face" is just another way of killing time.

"I ain't got nothin' else to do," the 16-year-old from New Haven's desolate Hill neighborhood explains, staring from beneath the brim of a black baseball cap.

"It kind of stinks, like something people in the hospital would use. They say they put it inside dead people," Villanueva said.

Villanueva was talking about what police believe is marijuana treated with embalming fluid. No one, not even William, is really sure.

On the streets, it goes by several names, "illie" and "ill face" among the most common. And since it made a sudden appearance in the region recently, it has become a popular, and probably poisonous, high for young people. It consists of a volatile mixture of formaldehyde, wood alcohol and other chemicals used to preserve dead bodies.

* * *

Cambridge, MA -- A man who tried to stage a fake Halloween hanging in a tavern, but wound up choking to death in front of unsuspecting patrons, "had a stupid look on his face like he was kidding around," a witness said.

Milton Tyree, 41, died when a harness he'd rigged to simulate a hanging at the Cantab Lounge slipped, choking him.

When he walked into the bar, Tyree had his face painted white, was wearing a black hood and carried a sickle "like the Grim Reaper," said witness Mike Dorman.

"He came in and stood up on a chair and hitched himself to a beam," Dorman said. "Somebody just pulled the chair out. He didn't look uncomfortable at all. He was moving his arms and everything. He always had a stupid look on his face like he was kidding around."

Said one police officer: "The harness slipped and he really was hanging, but it took the crowd a while to realize what was happening. When our officers arrived, he was down, someone had cut him down, but it was too late.'

Bar owner Rich Fitzgerald said he stopped Tyree from performing the trick earlier in the evening.

"He came in dressed like some kind of a creature and he had a noose around his neck with about a six-inch rope," Fitzgerald said. "He had this harness around his body, a kind of nylon net, which he lifted up his costume and showed me."

* * *

London -- A kamikaze grouse, shot during a hunting expedition in Scotland, glanced off the royal shoulder of Queen Elizabeth II causing a mild bruise.

The Queen, 69, shrieked when she was hit by the bird, but soon laughed it off.

* * *

Panama City -- A man attacked by a swarm of bees while fishing in Panama drowned when, his eyes swollen shut by the bee stings, he could not find his life jacket and jumped into a lake to escape the insects.

Gary E. Hauser, 42, was fishing with two friends in Gatun Lake in Panama, when the swarm descended on them. The three men jumped into the water and hung onto the boat, but the bees still swarmed over them. They got back into the boat to try to flee, but couldn't get the motor started. They went back into the water. Two swam to shore, but Hauser drowned.

* * *

Syracuse -- An 80-year-old golfer was crushed to death by his golf cart.

"He always said if he was going to go, he was going to go on a golf course, " his widow, Bertha, said. "He loved golf more than anything. I'm sure he died happy."

* * *

Baltimore -- After singing several robust choruses of "Please Don't Talk About Me When I'm Gone," an actress collapsed on stage for her death scene, and died of a heart attack.

Edith Webster, 60, who played the role of the grandmother in a performance of "The Drunkard" at the Towson Moose Lodge, fell to the stage amid applause from an audience of more than 200 and remained there as startled actors called for a doctor.

At first, the audience thought the calls for aid were part of the script, said director Richard Byrd. Afterward the audience sat quietly for almost an hour, and many prayed. The show did not continue.

Her daughter, Merri-Todd Webster, said the manner of her mother's death was "not a bad thing...a lot of people have been saying it. It's the first thing I thought of when I was at the hospital."

* * *

New York -- Three boys unwittingly used a wrapped-up human head as a soccer ball before the father of one of the youngsters realized what it was.

The head, found in the South Bronx, may belong to a torso discovered along a wooded area in Manhattan.

The boys, aged 9, 10 and 13, apparently pulled the head wrapped in rags out of a box of trash next to a fire hydrant on a dead end street.

"The kids started to play soccer with the object and then threw it into a trash can containing a fire," said police officer Mary Wrenson.

Ralph Rodriguez was washing his car at the hydrant. After the object went into the fire, Rodriguez noticed a leg sticking out of a garbage bag in the box and realized what the "ball" was.

He looked closer and found arms and legs.

* * *

Parma, Ohio -- A 23-year-old man wanted to be a realistic-looking Dracula for Halloween. All he needed was a stake in his heart.

So he drove a knife into a board which he had placed under his shirt. But the board cracked and knife pierced his chest. He died two hours later.

* * *

Darthmouth, Nova Scotia -- David Wayne Godin's bachelor party must have been fun. But it ended badly. Returning from the party, Godin's car plunged into a lake. When his body was retrieved, rescuers found him with an authentic ball and chain attached to his leg, courtesy of his friends at the party.

* * *

Seoul -- A South Korean fisherman was killed when the fish he caught stabbed him with his knife. After landing a large tuna, the fisherman began the process of cleaning the fish. Suddenly, it's tail flicked, sending the knife he was holding straight into his chest.

* * *

Quick Takes
-- On the 129-yard fourth hole at a golf course in Hemet, California, Peter Sedore hit a hole-in-one. On the next hole, he dropped dead.

-- Despite the fact that 200 lifeguards attended a New Orleans party, one guest drowned. The party was held to celebrate the first season that no one had drowned in the recreation department pool.

-- A vacationer at the French Riviera was killed when a runaway beach umbrella struck her in the chest as she lay sunbathing.

-- While playing badminton, a Malaysian man fell, knocking his dentures loose and causing him to suffocate.

-- Fifteen people dancing on bus roofs on the way to an election rally were killed when they became entangled in high voltage power lines.

-- When a rabbit-hunter laid down his gun to rest, he was shot dead by a rabbit which rushed from its burrow and bumped against the trigger.

HISTORIC PRESERVATION

Paducah, KY -- For a dead man, Henry "Speedy" Atkins gave people a lot of joy.

For 66 years his well-preserved corpse, used in an embalming experiment, was a tourist attraction at a funeral home in this Ohio River town.

Townsfolk and the occasional bus load of out-of-towners gawked at his mummified body, which was stored propped against a closet wall and carefully washed and dressed three times a year to keep mold off.

But finally, the people who cared for Speedy decided it was time for him to be laid to rest.

* * *

Deluth, Minn -- When feuding relatives got together to settle the estate of a deceased family member, they discovered their reclusive mother had also died about a year earlier.

The death of Blanche Hansen was discovered when her son, Robert Hansen, asked his brother-in-law, Ken Evenson, "So where are you keeping Mom?"

The question puzzled Evenson who replied, "We thought you were taking care of her."

In fact, no one had taken care of Hansen, 80, whose body was discovered by relatives in the living room of her locked bungalow, the day after the estate of Harold Hansen, 82, Blanche's brother, brought them together.

Authorities say she died at least a year earlier and possibly longer.

"It sounds dumb, but that's what happened," Evenson said of the estrangement among Hansen and her two children, Carol Evenson and Robert Hansen. "We feel awful about it."

"She was just lying there, what was left of her, wearing a bathrobe and a sweater," Officer Brad Crandall said.

Evenson said his wife and her brother had avoided contact with each other since an argument several years ago about the family's lake cabin. He also said the mother shunned contact with both her children, telling her daughter not to bring her children over anymore.

Evenson said Mrs. Hansen's life as a recluse apparently began with a "nervous breakdown" after the birth of her daughter, who "had to kind of look after herself while growing up." The woman's husband refused to have her committed and looked after her himself until he died, Evenson said. "Her drapes were always closed," neighbor Beverly La Plante said. "We assumed she was living with her daughter or in a nursing home, but were never sure because there was always smoke coming out of her chimney."

* * *

New York -- A doctor's mistake. Car thieves. A protective and curious cabbie. Put them together in Manhattan's East Village and you've got the tale of an errant box of partially dissected human heads.

The cabbie found the six heads in a box in the gutter, said Officer Scott Bloch.

Dr. William Portney of New York Eye and Ear Infirmary decided to leave the carton in the back of his hatchback when he parked in the East Village.

Portney was transporting the partial heads, the backs were cut away but the faces left intact, to the New York Medical College in Valhalla from his New York Hospital for a class in medical dissection.

Thieves broke into Portney's car and stole what they apparently thought was marketable booty.

* * *

Maple Heights, Ohio -- An 83-year-old woman found mummified in the house she shared with her son died of natural causes two years earlier.

The woman's son, Herbert Loser, 58, was arrested on a misdemeanor charge of failure to report a corpse. Loser indicated that his only income was his mother's Social Security checks.

Loser told neighbors his mother was alive, but they became concerned after not seeing her and notified authorities. When social workers would call, Loser would carry on pretend conversations with his mother.

* * *

Los Angeles -- A woman was sentenced to 15 years in prison for allowing her quadriplegic husband to rot to death.

A judge recounted testimony from medical workers who described Scott Mickler's condition at his wife's trial; an overpowering stench as he lay in a bed covered with flesh and body wastes, gangrene so severe that his toes and heels were falling off.

Cheryl Mickler was convicted of abuse or neglect of a disabled adult. A quadriplegic since a 1978 car crash, her husband had won a $3.5 million settlement and she ended up with $1.5 million after he died.

* * *

Los Angeles -- Before his death, Sixties drug guru Timothy Leary said he signed up to have his head removed and frozen after he dies for possible resurrection, but he admitted that the technology was "a long shot."

"I don't want to just go belly-up when my Blue Cross runs out," said the former Harvard psychology professor, who once advised the youth of America to "tune in, turn on and drop out" with mind-altering drugs.

Leary said he formalized a $35,000 agreement to have his head preserved for posterity in so-called cryonics suspension by the Alcor Life Extension Foundation in Riverside.

"It's the second dumbest idea in the world," Leary said of cryonics, the practice of freezing the recently dead. "The first is that you go to the worms. It's a long shot, but it's worth a try."

Alcor is best known for a long-running battle with authorities about whether an elderly woman client was actually dead when her head was surgically severed and immersed in liquid nitrogen.

For his $35,000, Leary, who was perfectly healthy at the time, would become a member of the non-profit Alcor Foundation. That gives him the right to have his head surgically removed after his death and immersed in liquid nitrogen at minus 320 degrees Fahrenheit.

* * *

London -- A preserved and tattooed head of a Maori warrior was put up for auction, then withdrawn after protests by the New Zealand Maori Council.

The British woman who wanted to sell the full-size head, expected to fetch up to $7,000, received a hand-carved Maori club in exchange.

The head is mounted on a platter.

* * *

Galesburg, Ill. -- Two children tended their father's corpse for 8-1/2 years in hopes he'd revive.

"The children told me they did not believe their father was dead," said detective Steven Johnson. "They said his presence is still in the house, and they still can communicate with him."

Carol Stevens, a 42-year-old registered nurse, and her companion, Richard Kunce, 56, were charged with felony forgery for trying to gain access to the bank account of the dead man, Carl Stevens. Mrs. Stevens said that her husband "expired" in her arms on May 12, 1979.

ON THE EDGE

Tokyo -- Police arrested a fisherman and his cousin for trying to feed the fisherman's wife to sharks after an argument. The fisherman threw his wife into a net and dragged her behind his boat in shark-infested waters for about half-an-hour. "I will use you as bait for the sharks," he said.

* * *

Bristol, CT -- A cabinet maker was impaled in the groin when a 10-foot splinter hit him while he was operating a saw.

Michael Labbe, 29, was impaled when the wood "kicked back" while he was performing a routine operation with a saw.

* * *

Lancaster, SC -- A man who tried to use a gun as a hammer instead shot himself and his wife on Christmas night.

The man's mother-in-law, Molly Goodman, said she asked him to repair the hallway molding. When he couldn't push it back into place with his hands, he went into the living room and got a .25 caliber handgun.

Richard Gardner, 23, shot himself in the hand and his wife, Mary Ann Gardner, 21, in the abdomen.

* * *

Milwaukee -- A man cut his girlfriend's neck with a knife and tried to suck blood from her wounds after watching a vampire movie on New Year's Eve.

The man apparently became upset after Dracula died.

Stephen J. Wilhelm, 35, was charged with recklessly endangering safety while armed on Katherine Zielski, 30.

* * *

Milwaukee -- A 300-pound woman nearly smothered her husband by sitting on him during a dispute. The man was hospitalized in critical condition and the woman was arrested.

The man had threatened to get a gun during an argument Friday when his wife pushed him to the ground and sat on his head and chest, cutting off his breathing.

The couple's two children helped hold the man.

* * *

Portland, Maine -- A high school athlete said he reacted on adrenaline when a 10-foot javelin punctured his abdomen, passed though a kidney and got stuck in his back.

"I had trouble breathing. I felt I was going to die, " he said.

* * *

Nairobi -- A 2-year-old child was saved from the mouth of a 10-foot-long python after being swallowed to the waste.

The child's mother and other villagers had fled from the reptile, but a watchman attacked the snake with a sharp stone so that it regurgitated the victim unharmed.

The reptile was then beaten to death.

* * *

Newton, PA -- A man planting mums on his mother's grave was trapped for two hours when the ground gave way and he sank knee-high.

Ken McLaughlin, 29, said he tried to free himself, but the leg that sank into soft ground became stuck under the base of his mother's headstone.

Help arrived after two hours. "I screamed and shouted for help, but nobody came. I was really upset," he said.

* * *

Quick Takes

-- A man in Brazil nearly killed himself when he tried to stop his toothache by biting a bullet. The bullet exploded.

-- A thirsty man almost died when he swallowed porcupine quills which his son had been saving in a glass of water.

-- A Seattle man nearly died when he fell out of his back door. He forgot that he removed his back porch two weeks earlier.

-- A drunken woman nearly killed herself when she tried to remove a callus from her foot with a shotgun.

ALL CHOKED UP

Budapest, Hungary -- An 80-year-old woman bent into a sauerkraut barrel to scoop out a portion, but fell in and drowned.

Julianna Farkas, a Hungarian from Romania, was visiting relatives east of Budapest. Neighbors discovered the accident when they heard the woman's 3-year-old great-grandson crying in the yard with no one attending to him. The woman apparently became dizzy as she leaned over the barrel, which was in a shed, and was overcome by the pungent fumes. The liquid in the barrel was 12 inches deep.

London -- A gang who tossed vegetables at pedestrians was implicated in the death of a man who was killed after being hit by a turnip that was thrown from a passing car.

Another man suffered stomach injuries after being hit by a cabbage.

"It sounds very amusing, but clearly it is not because a man has died. We are treating this very seriously indeed," the police said.

* * *

Bangalore, India -- At least 16 people died and 630 became ill after eating the decomposed meat of animals sacrificed during a Hindu ritual.

About 8,000 devotees ate the meat of 250 sheep and goats and fell ill. The carcasses were covered with blood and were left outdoors for about 24 hours before eaten.

Worshippers chanted prayers to complete the ritual, which is suppose to prevent natural calamities.

* * *

Ketchum, Idaho -- A man died after a beer keg in his refrigerator ruptured, shot upward and hit him in the head.

Clinton Doan, 35, died when he opened the refrigerator in his garage to put his lunch for the next day inside.

When the refrigerator opened, the bottom of the keg cracked, shooting the keg upward "like a missile," said sheriff's deputy Gene Ramsey.

"The magnitude of the explosion was just tremendous."

* * *

Atlanta -- Desire cost four men their lives when they swallowed dried toad secretions, a purported aphrodisiac sold at grocery stores and tobacco shops.

The brown, rock-like substance causes hallucinations. It is suppose to be applied to the genitals, but wasn't labeled.

The would-be Romeos who ingested it began vomiting and their hearts beat erratically, not from lust but from the love potion.

There are no safe substances proven to have aphrodisiac effects, although the belief that something works can be powerful, officials said.

* * *

Boston -- A nurse was cleared of wrongdoing in the death of a retarded man who ate more than two pounds of paper towels.

"I'm glad the state has decided to end this ordeal and will fulfill its obligation to me," Valerie Johnson said.

Johnson, 54, who was day supervisor at the John T. Barry Rehabilitation Center in North Reading, was fired after an investigation concluded she did not treat the man's condition as an emergency.

* * *

Princeton, W.V. -- Workers found a decomposed body in a water tank after residents complained their water smelled and tasted foul.

"It was really, really bad," said 16-year-old David Woolwine. "Even when it wasn't looking bad, it smelled."

"I think I'll drink bottled water for a while," said resident Pat Veneri.

* * *

Harrisville, W.V. -- The man who killed a local funeral director for licking food off his body was found not guilty of murder.

The funeral director spread mayonnaise, ketchup, mustard and pickle juice on the sleeping man and began to lick it off his nude body. When the man awoke, he stabbed the funeral director 13 times.

The court found that the killer was temporarily insane because of the circumstances.

* * *

Chico, CA -- A man was arrested for stealing people's ashes from a cemetery in hopes of attaining "everlasting life."

Rodney Hines, 36, claimed he snorted some of the ashes and sprinkled them on his food because he wanted to live forever.

Police said they were led to Hines by an acquaintance who had told them Hines was bragging about having human ashes.

* * *

Murmansk, Russia -- Nearly 100 people died from drinking homemade vodka -- some of it distilled in a former pigpen.

Murmansk police seized about 50 tons of illegally made vodka in one raid, part of a crackdown on moonshiners.

More than 700 people in the city of 412,000 were hospitalized in one year with acute alcohol poisoning after drinking the bad brew.

* * *

Quick Takes

-- A 22-year-old Toronto man choked to death on an 874 page pocket Bible that he tried to swallow in order to purge himself of the Devil.

-- An insurance executive was charged with tearing out his wife's heart and lungs and impaling them on a stake in a fight about overcooked ziti.

-- Four boys died shortly after eating soup in which their mother had inadvertently cooked a poisonous snake.

-- A woman laughed so hard at her grandson's new haircut, that she choked to death on the candy she was eating.

UNDERHANDED UNDERTAKINGS

Cambridge, MA -- Apparently death pays.

According to a study an economic research firm, the best managerial job in the country is a funeral director.

The survey ranked job prospects in 219 traditional industries, comparing their pay, growth potential and security.

Runners-up for the best management jobs are in advertising and drug manufacturing.

Cognetics noted in its report that job security takes a high priority. It estimates about one-quarter of all-American employees are dismissed from their companies about every four years. So finding a job that lasts can be just as important as finding a job that pays well.

* * *

Miami -- Eastern Airlines offered discounts and frequent-flier mileage to funeral homes who used the carrier to ship bodies.

The special cargo rate for shipping the deceased was just one of many incentives the airline offered in an attempt to regain customers lost in a month-long strike.

"It's just a whole scheme of rebuilding an airline from scratch," he said. "We had been out of many markets for some time, and when returning to those markets we were using price as an incentive to get some of them back."

Eastern cargo officials made personal visits to funeral homes, offering a 50 percent discount on transportation of corpses and frequent-flier mileage to funeral home operators for their shipments.

* * *

Riverside, CA -- When fumes coming from a patient's body knocked out a doctor and a nurse, hospital officials were forced to close the emergency room.

While the patient was in cardiac arrest in Riverside General Hospital, the doctor and nurse drew a blood sample, noticed white crystals in the blood and smelled an odor like ammonia. Then they passed out. The patient died.

"It appears to be something coming from the body itself," said an investigator. "We are trying to get background before we approach the body. We don't want to put more people at risk."

Coroner's officials were consulting doctors to figure out what happened, and an autopsy was pending. No one was aware of any similar cases.

The 31-year-old female patient had been undergoing home chemotherapy treatment for cancer.

* * *

Los Angeles -- Now for the ultimate air trip.

A California company is offering what it calls a "traveler retrieval service." If you die more than 100 miles from home, Above and Beyond will bring your body home, sending a private aircraft to Katmandu if that's what it takes.

The service includes handling red tape wherever it is that you may die, and taking at least two and perhaps as many as five family members along to accompany the body home. The price is a one-time fee of $249 until you reach age 60. After that it is $299.

* * *

Ovalau -- The mortuary cooler on the tropical island of Ovalau in the Pacific Ocean hadn't worked for a year, and some mourners were asked to bring ice to preserve the bodies of loved ones before burial or cremation.

The cooler hadn't been fixed despite a $7,200 government grant, and families were being told to cremate their dead within 24 hours.

Those who delay were asked to bring their own ice. "We are not happy," said Peni Bakana, chairman of the provincial council at Levuka on Ovalau.

* * *

Allentown, PA -- Dear Ms. Lazer: In case you didn't know it already, you're dead.

"You died Aug. 30, 1990, and have no survivors," said a letter sent by the Human Relations Commission in Allentown, PA, to Diane Lazer.

The commission told Lazer, who died at age 44 when a gas explosion leveled her house, that it was closing her employment claim against Lehigh County Prison.

It reminded her that she still can sue the county, and advised her to seek an attorney's help. If she has questions, it said, she can call City Hall.

Nicholas Butterfield, the human relations officer who wrote this letter, said he hadn't heard from Lazer yet.

"To be honest with you," he said, "I don't expect a reply."

So why write a letter to a dead woman telling her that she is dead, and send it to a house that was reduced to rubble?

Official duty.

"We're trying to notify an estate that we're closing a case," Butterfield said. "The intent was not to reach the dead woman. The intent was to reach the estate."

The letter responds to a complaint Lazer made in 1988, the year she left her work as a prison guard.

After the letter was mailed, Butterfield's supervisor, Raymond C. Polaski, ordered a second, almost identical letter sent to the Lazer's estate.

The estate's address?

"I have no idea," Butterfield said. "I sent it to the same address."

* * *

Tampa -- US Air is offering funeral directors a free round-trip ticket for every 30 bodies they ship.

"The shipment of human remains has become a very big business," said Angela Burris, USAir district sales manager for cargo in Tampa, FL "We want to get a part of that business."

Since initiating the so-called TLC program, the airline has had a 30 percent increase in the number of bodies shipped.

But USAir spokesman Mike Clark said that he did not know of anyone collecting a freebie yet for booking bodies.

Shipping a body costs $68 to $635, depending on the weight and the distance flown. There is no extra charge to send a spray of flowers.

Florida, like other Sun Belt states, ranks high in such shipments because of all the retirees from the north who want to be buried back home. Human remains are the second most popular cargo from Tampa, behind tropical fish.

* * *

North Adams, Mass. -- David Champagne and Robert Whipple wanted to revive the rage for bronzed baby shoes. But customers didn't bite.

Until one showed up with the skull of a 260-pound black bear. He said... "I want to bronze it for my stepmother " Champagne recalled Tuesday. "I said 'Sure you do! "

But he really did.

So, with a shrug and a philosopher's "why not," a new business was born: Metal-Heads by Mr. Whipple's Bronzing.

Champagne and Whipple, buddies who used to work in construction, now bronze animal skulls as trophies for proud hunters or display pieces for taxidermists and outfitters.

Heartened by the budding bull market, they plated about 30 skulls in their first few months, including that of a fox, wild boar and turtle.

In a process akin to making candles, a skull is dipped into a liquid mix of pulverized metal and resins. Over three days, the coating hardens into a molded shell that, if handled carefully, will last and last.

At $10 an inch measured over a skull's length and height, a medium-sized bear skull mounted on wood costs less than $200, Champagne said.

Taxidermist Rick LaBlue of nearby Adams bought a bear skull for display at his business and another for his father who had bagged his first bear.

"I think it gives it more of a finished look, more of something that you would put on your mantel, something that gives a little class," said his wife, Phyllis, who helps run the business.

* * *

Los Angeles -- The Los Angeles County Coroner's Office has its own little shop of horrors, where it markets the morbid, from personalized toe tags to skeleton tote bags. There's even a beach towel with a child body outline.

Proceeds from the gift shop, Skeletons in the Closet, go to a program aimed at scaring youths out of drinking and driving.

"Bodies and death are our business. We're just trying to take advantage of it," said Marilyn Lewis, the coroner's new marketing program coordinator.

* * *

Frankfurt -- A macabre problem is worrying Greman cemetery administrators: their corpses aren't rotting. They remain miraculously preserved for years on end.

Often thought among Catholics to be an indication of saintliness, incorruption of buried human remains has scientific grounds well-known to gravediggers.

If the soil is particularly dry, a body will end up naturally mummified. Extremely wet soils also retard decay, producing a corpse with a waxy appearance.

The phenomenon would not have become a political issue if it hadn't been for Germany's land shortage. Eternal peace in German soil can be brief: Graves are rented out for a limited term and are allowed to be dug up as little as 15 years after burial. When the lease runs out and the body has decomposed, the grave is offered again to the public by cemetery operators.

Germans perceive no disrespect to the dead in this practice, which saves cemeteries from having to continually expand as more people die.

"Very slow decay or none at all" is a known feature of certain graveyards in Germany.

* * *

Quick Takes

-- Solar-powered tombstones are now available from a California company. The grave markers repeat recorded messages to graveside visitors.

-- In New Jersey, a police officer ordered the opening of a grave to retrieve the hat he had loaned the grieving family for the wake.

MISTAKEN IDENTITY

Guiginto, Philippines -- Nardo San Diego was surprised to find a wake under way at his home when he returned from visiting a friend.

"Who died?" he asked.

"You," a startled friend replied.

The mix-up began when San Diego, an alderman in this town near Manila, left to visit a friend in another province.

That same day, police found a body lying on the road near the town and mistakenly identified it as San Diego's.

They turned the body, which strongly resembled the alderman, over to his mother, who then organized the traditional nine-day wake at the deceased's home.

On the third day of the wake, San Diego returned home to the surprise of the mourners.

* * *

Norway, Maine -- The Selective Service System says it would apologize to Luther Pike if it could for sending him a notice that he had better sign up for the draft or face a jail sentence.

The problem is, Pike is dead. And if he were alive, he would have been 118 years old when he got the government's letter.

Pike, in his day a well-known businessman in this western Maine town, was born on Sept. 9, 1877. But because of a typographical error somewhere along the line, the government recorded him as being born in 1977.

* * *

Tyler, Texas -- Hearing he was dead wasn't the way James Rippard had expected to start his work day, but it gave him the chance to enjoy his wake.

Rippard's co-workers at a Tyler foundry heard that the 54-year-old man had been killed in a car accident. Rippard, however, didn't learn of his "death" until he showed up for work the next day.

"People kept telling me, 'Hey man, you're supposed to be dead,' " Rippard said. "I told them, 'If I'm dead, I don't know what the hell I'm doing here working.' "

Police officers had determined through identification papers found on a man's body that Rippard died in a car accident west of Tyler. The victim was later identified as Virgil Murray, 34, who was wanted on felony warrants in Tennessee.

Patricia Parvin, Murray's common-law wife, identified the dead man as Rippard, leading investigators to believe Murray had been using Rippard's name as an alias.

But after talking with Rippard and finding a "Virgil Loves Diane" tattoo on the victim's body, troopers were willing to admit the mistake and Rippard was officially back among the living.

* * *

Stamford, CT -- A medical training doll found along a darkened roadside was too realistic for an assistant medical examiner: He mistook it for an aborted, partially frozen fetus and declared it dead.

Police found the doll after a passerby called. It was covered with sand and gravel and one of it's arms were severed.

Assistant Medical Examiner Henry Minot was called to the scene, and sent the tiny body to the state office of the Chief Medical Examiner in Farmington for an autopsy.

Minot said both he and police were fooled. "This was obviously something that had been at the side of the road through a snowstorm... and it looked enough like a fetus so that we thought it was," Minot said.

The state's chief medical examiner, Dr. Wayne Carver, said the silicon rubber doll was a training mannequin made to resemble an anatomically correct fetus.

He does not consider what Minot did a mistake. "I'd much rather he did this than call it a mannequin and be wrong," Carver said.

Carver said his office receives four or five cases a month in which police are unable to determine whether they have found human remains. A doll made it to his office at least one other time.

Norfolk, Va. -- While friends and relatives attended his graveside service, Charles Pryor rested in his hospital bed, unaware that another man was being buried in a cemetery plot intended for him.

Authorities said they didn't know who was buried in Pryor's grave, and they were not sure how such a case of mistaken identity could occur.

A few hours after a man believed to be Pryor was buried in Hampton National Cemetery, two of his relatives were escorted by curious officials to a ward at the Veterans Administration Hospital in Hampton, near the cemetery. They identified a patient there as Pryor.

Pryor, 61, had checked into the hospital for an undisclosed ailment, the day a newspaper ran his obituary. The relatives, a brother and niece, were summoned after a hospital employee read the obituary and noticed similarities to the history of a patient.

State Medical Examiner Faruk Presswalla said Pryor's half-brother viewed the body of the dead man and identified it as that of Pryor. Also, family members viewed the body at the funeral. He said the fact that family members saw the body makes the mix-up especially mystifying.

"The family saw the body at the funeral home," Presswalla said. "So why this has happened, I don't know. It's an error, but it's really an error within the family, not the medical examiner's office or the police."

Pryor was unaware of the mix-up. "I don't know anything about that," he said. "I don't have a brother."

A nurse said he was too confused to talk. She said he could not receive visitors.

* * *

Oklahoma City -- The funeral home had been notified. A list of pallbearers was half done. The family had been mourning for hours when the call came: Jim Snodgrass was alive.

"We all looked like ghosts. We just stood there," daughter Terri Crawford said.

The family had received a call from an Oklahoma City hospital where her 59-year-old father was an ulcer patient. He apparently died of a heart attack.

"We were in the middle of making a list of pallbearers when the hospital called back and apologized, telling us they had made a terrible mistake," Crawford said.

It turned out that another patient with the same last name and middle initial had died.

"We did an awful lot of grieving for that man," she said.

ZAPPED AT THE ZOO

Copenhagen, Denmark -- Opera may be sweet to some people's ears, but to one animal, the strains of Wagner were fatal.

At the Copenhagen Zoo, one of its okapis, a rare African mammal related to the giraffe, died from stress triggered by opera singers rehearsing 300 yards away in a park.

The 6-year-old okapis collapsed after Royal Theater performers began singing selections from Tannhauser. "She started hyperventilating, went into shock and collapsed," said a zookeeper.

* * *

Belgrade, Yugoslavia -- A zebra at the Sarajevo Zoo chose death over captivity and killed herself by smashing her head against the ground.

The zebra broke her spine after keepers foiled an attempt by her and her mate to escape.

* * *

Los Angeles -- A giant octopus was found dead in an empty tank at the Cabrillo Marine Aquarium after the animal pulled out a drain pipe during the night.

"We thought for sure that this would be well beyond her capabilities," said a spokesman.

The 58-pound octopus with 12-foot arms was in a 600-gallon tank.

* * *

Moscow -- Kolya, a crocodile whose life began in the era of the czars, has finally died. He survived two world wars, a revolution and a civil war to become Russia's oldest known crocodile.

Officials say the 9-foot, 10-inch crocodile, the largest in Russia, was probably in captivity when the Bolsheviks executed Russia's last czar, Nicholas II, there in 1918.

Zoo curator Natalya Bobkoskaya said Kolya showed up in Yekaterinburg between 1913 and 1915 when he was part of an animal show that toured the region. He was already full-grown, which made him between 110-115 years old when he died.

* * *

Copenhagen, Denmark -- Frederik the elephant, who had been pestered for years by seven aggressive she-elephants, has died of a heart attack brought on by stress.

"It was as if he'd given up hope for a decent life after the rough treatment he suffered at the hands of his wives recently," said Leif Nielsen, director of the Giskud Lion Park Zoo in Jutland.

Nielsen said that three of the female elephants with whom Frederik had shared a yard for years ganged up on him and shoved him into a pond.

"Frederik had always been a bit frail," said Nielsen. "He couldn't fend for himself and never recovered from his bout in the pond."

Every time Frederik tried to turn his amorous attentions to one female, the others would mob him out of jealousy. The zoo is considering acquiring a new, more robust male elephant who can cope with the females and sire offspring.

* * *

New York -- Ellie, a circus elephant with Ringling Brothers, was electrocuted as she erected a circus tent.
The fatal jolt occurred when the tent pole she was lifting came in contact with a power line. As she collapsed, Ellie crushed her trainer to death.

SERVES YOU RIGHT

Moscow -- A tiger that had not been fed for five days escaped from it's cage in a zoo in the far Eastern city of Vladiyostok and devoured one of it's keepers.
The tiger was later shot to death by the keeper's husband.
As the economic situation worsened throughout Russia, humans weren't the only ones to suffer. Zoo and circus animals were also forced to put up with poor diets and infrequent feedings.

***

Anchorage, Alaska -- A man was stomped to death at the University of Alaska by a moose that was being harassed by students as it roamed the campus with it's calf.

The animals were outside the gym when 71-year-old Myong Chin Ra arrived to use the sauna.

"There were people standing around throwing snowballs, yelling, whistling, shouting, trying to get their attention." said Ann Gross.

The moose charged, and Ra ran, falling on a slippery walkway. He was stomped about a dozen times. The animals were allowed to leave the campus into nearby woods.

***

Middletown, Ohio -- During gun control activist Sarah Brady's speech here, she was shouted down by protesters. But the loudest heckler of them all had a heart attack mid-yell.

John Luckett, 70, of West Chester, collapsed in his seat among the crowd of 600 people.

"At first I think everyone thought he was okay, that he was just clowning," Becker said. When it became clear that Luckett was ill, he was taken to Middletown Regional Hospital, where he was pronounced dead of an apparent heart attack.

* * *

Sumpter Township, Mich. -- A man was killed after apparently tripping a shotgun booby trap he had set to protect marijuana plants in his garage.

Ken Sutherland, 38, bled to death from a thigh wound. After he was shot, he dragged himself 60 feet to his kitchen and dialed 911 twice, but was unable to say anything. Police traced the call and found Sutherland unconscious and bleeding.

Police found a shotgun nailed to a chair with a wire stretched from the trigger to an outer screen door. The gun was meant to fire when the door was opened. About 20 to 30 marijuana plants were found in the garage.

* * *

Enigma, GA -- A man died after being bitten by a rattlesnake which he had taken to church because the Bible says believers "shall take up serpents."

Dewey Bruce Hal, 40, was bitten during services at New River Free Holiness Church and died at home. He refused medical treatment.

Martha Hale, a cousin of the victim, said church members take the Bible literally. "Many have been bitten and were healed at that church." she said. "They feel he didn't die because of the snake, but that he died because it was his time to go."

* * *

Harrare, Zimbabwe -- A man who sneaked into a wild animal park to steal meat was caught and devoured by lions.

The intruder's remains were found by a warden at the Lion and Cheetah Park.

"He got into a cage with four very bad lions," Vivian Bristow, owner of the park, said. She said that the man was believed to have entered the cage to steal meat left for the animals. There are 32 lions at the park.

All that remained of the man were bones.

IMPLEMENTS OF DESTRUCTION?

Kuala Lumpur, Malaysia -- A farmer was killed when a coconut, thrown by his pet monkey, hit him in the neck.

Mat Hussin Sulaiman, 76, was waiting below a tree to collect the coconuts that his monkey was trained to pluck when he broke his neck.

Trained monkeys are widely used in Malaysia to climb coconut trees to pluck the fruit. The animals are leashed, and twist the nuts vigorously until they break free.

They usually drop, rather than throw, the coconuts they pick.

* * *

Toledo, Ohio -- A man was convicted of involuntary manslaughter for stuffing a Nerf ball down a man's throat to keep him quiet while he was being fondled.

Dearsman, 54, confessed to killing Wetzel and drew a map that led police to the body. He testified that he never meant to hurt Wetzel and tried to resuscitate him.

* * *

Green Bay, Wis. -- Six paper mill workers were convicted of murdering a police informant found in a vat of paper pulp with a 50-pound weight tied around his neck.

The six turned on Thomas Monfils for calling police about a plan to steal an extension cord from the James River Corp. mill where they worked.

They were convicted of being a party to first-degree murder for beating up Monfils out of revenge and anger, then dumping him in the vat of mud-like paper pulp after they realized he was badly hurt.

Monfils, 35, suffocated in the vat.

* * *

Phoenix -- Guided by a premonition, Christina Black stuffed a kiwi fruit down her 88-year-old grandmother's throat, killing the old woman.

Police and Helen Gerstung's long-time doctor initially concluded the woman had died of natural causes. But once Gerstung was buried, her granddaughter called authorities and told them what she had done.

Ten months after Gerstung's death, Black, a 35-year-old Orlando, FL, woman with a history of mental illness, was in court in Orlando. According to police, Black accompanied her grandmother to Apache Junction, a Phoenix suburb where the old woman rented a trailer.

A day later, Gerstung was dead. An autopsy found kiwi seeds in her mouth and pieces of fruit in her throat.

* * *

Sydney, Australia -- A millionaire took an overdose of sleeping pills so he wouldn't have to listen to his grandchildren playing Frank Sinatra's "My Way" any more.

The grandchildren, his only survivors, intentionally drove Donald Gruner mad so they could get their hands on his money.

Gruner had been locked in his bedroom for 101 days with "My Way" playing 24 hours. Police uncovered the plot when one of the relatives had regrets and confessed.

"They knew he didn't like Sinatra's voice, so they drove him mad to inherit his money," said a police detective.

"Their plan was to destroy the old man with psychological torture. Unfortunately, we can't charge them. He committed suicide and there's no evidence of foul play."

* * *

Quick Takes

-- In Paris, a grocer murdered his wife with a wedge of parmesan cheese, while in New Zealand a man used frozen sausage to kill his wife.

-- Two Brazilian sailors were killed in a naval battle in the 1800s when an Uruguayan ship ran out of ammunition and shot cheese from its cannon. The cheese broke the Brazilian ship's mast, which killed the sailors.

SUCCUMBING TO SEX

Huntsville, Ala. -- Huntsville police charged a man with manslaughter after the woman who was performing fellatio on him choked to death.

According to his attorney, "It was an oral sex act, and the girl died. Well, what is his crime?"

A grand jury later decided not to indict.

* * *

San Francisco -- A nightclub manager was crushed to death against a ceiling by a piano while having sex.

James Ferrozzo, assistant manager of the Condor Club, was crushed to death when a piano on which he was having sex with the club's star stripper rose from the floor on an electric pulley and pinned him to the ceiling.

Ferrozzo accidentally turned on the piano's elevator switch during an after-hours affair.

Since the piano rises very slowly on the pulley, the couple didn't even notice that they were rising.

The stripper sustained only bruises, but it took the fire department rescuers nearly three hours to free her from under Ferrozzo.

* * *

Bangkok -- A man blew himself up by inserting an air hose in his rectum and turning it on in a practice called pumping.

"The government must crack down on this disgusting craze," said a hospital spokesman. "If this perversion catches on, it will destroy the cream of Thailand's manhood."

Most pumpers use a standard bicycle pump to give themselves a sexually satisfying rush of air.

Chamchai Puanmuangpak started using a two-cylinder foot pump, but decided that wasn't exciting enough. So he boasted to friends that he was going to try the hose at a nearby gas station.

Not realizing how powerful the machine is, he inserted the hose in his rectum and inserted a one bath coin in the slot. Concluding the spokesman, "Inflate your tires by all means, but hide your bicycle pump where it cannot tempt you."

* * *

Orense, Spain -- Hermimio Rivera Concerio, a 39-year-old bricklayer, abducted a hen and climbed down a riverbank to consummate his passion. But in doing so, he dislodged a large rock, causing the granite boulder to crash down and kill him.

The pathologist later revealed that the man's penis was covered in feathers.

* * *

Quick Takes

-- A transvestite was run over by a train after he tied himself to the tracks to masturbate, but was unable to untie himself in time.

-- An Ohio woman spent four days underneath a man who died after they had sex in the front seat of her car. "I just thought he was a hard sleeper," she said.

-- When a man discovered that his wife was having an affair, he glued her hand to the lover's penis with acrylic cement. Toxic poisoning from the cement later killed her lover.

AIRING OUT

Paducah, Ky. -- A man who tried to hitch a ride on the wing of a commuter plane lost his grip shortly after takeoff and plunged 300 feet to his death.

The man grabbed on to the Northwest Airline plane after jumping a fence at Barkley Regional Airport and running across a field. The plane was traveling at about 150 mph when he fell.

* * *

Knoxville, Tenn. -- A parachutist carrying 77 pounds of cocaine around his waist plummeted to his death because the drug-laden duffel bags became entangled in his reserve chute.

Andrew Carter Thornton fell to his death from an altitude of about 7,000 feet when his main chute failed to open.

* * *

Paris -- An unexpected visitor dropped by Bernard and Denise Bisson's garden, a dead body.

A man's corpse came hurtling to the ground at the couple's home just north of Paris. Police believe the man, who was carrying 55 Russian rubles but no identification papers, was a Russian stowaway aboard an airplane.

* * *

Phoenix, Ariz. -- A glider pilot was killed when a 20-foot-tall cactus landed on his sail plane after one of it's wings struck the plant during a landing.

Seth Daniels, 35, of Carefree was landing when the glider swerved, possibly because of a wind gust, and one of it's wings sheared off the top of the cactus.

* * *

Louisburg, NC -- A tired parachutist's fatigue and his preoccupation with videotaping other jumpers led him to leap from a plane without a chute, plummeting 10,500 feet to his death.

The death of Ian Lester McGuire was accidental, although "a man who has jumped 800 times ought to remember his parachute," said the local sheriff.

McGuire, 35, was carrying a video camera mounted on his helmet and was filming an instructor and a student at Franklin County Sports Parachute Center. The videotape was mangled in the crash, but salvaged by investigators.

The videotape showed that McGuire jumped from the airplane and the jump was going smoothly until the parachutes worn by the instructor and the student deployed and McGuire hurtled below them.

"It kind of appears he reached for his parachute and didn't have one," Brown said. "You could only see the instructor and the student falling on the video. But the release for his parachute is to his right hip, and when that right hand goes down, the left hand comes forward and it comes into camera view."

"Then the pictures get to moving real fast because he's approaching the ground at 150 mph. The only thing the camera shows is the ground coming."

* * *

Denver -- A jetliner carrying 205 people made an unscheduled landing to remove two coffins from the cargo hold after passengers complained they were overcome by offensive odors.

The pilot of United's Flight 686 from Las Vegas to Chicago requested permission to make the landing at Stapleton International Airport after passengers complained of dizziness and breathing trouble on the plane.

"I have heard there was a powder material they put in (coffins for air transport), " said the pilot. "Apparently it was not working."

After the coffins were removed, the Boeing 767 was aired out and the flight resumed about an hour later.

ODD ANIMAL EPITAPHS

Stockholm -- A Swedish farmer sued the owner of a local golf course after claiming that a field littered with errant golf balls caused the death of her cows.

Cows grazing on land at Svinnersbo near Vastervik mistook the plastic-coated rubber balls for something to eat, said farmer Anne-Mari Johansson.

Until one of her charges dropped dead after a sudden seizure, she thought the biggest danger was getting hit by flying golf balls. A neighbor pointed out that the balls were lying all over Mrs. Johansson's meadow.

She took a policeman to the autopsy, where the veterinarian found several golf balls stuck in the stomach and esophagus of the dead cow. They had blocked the passage of digestive gases, causing the cow's death. Shortly after the diagnosis, a second cow dropped dead with the same symptoms.

* * *

London -- One of the world's rarest falcons, rescued from near-extinction by a wildlife charity, ate one of the world's rarest pigeons.

The drama took place on the Ile Aux Aigrettes, off the coast of Mauritius. The falcon was a Mauritius kestrel, whose numbers in the wild 18 years ago had fallen to just four and which was the world's rarest bird. But a breeding program has raised its numbers to 250.

In the last 12 years, the wildlife charity also ran a breeding program to increase the numbers of Mauritius pink pigeons, which were dying out due to deforestation and new predators such as monkeys and rats.

With the pigeons numbering up to 250, the charity began reintroducing them to the wild, but as the first chicks began to hatch, the kestrel swooped down and ate one of the young.

* * *

Enfield, NY -- A 4-year-old Chihuahua died while trying to protect her owner's property after a burglar threw the dog into a clothes dryer and turned it on.

"I don't see how anybody could do that," said Cynthia Furman, who found her dog, Tiny, in the dryer when she came home for lunch.

She said the family's other dog, a 6-year-old Springer Spaniel named Bagel, was cowering in the corner of the laundry room with scrapes on it's stomach.

Tompkins County Sheriff's deputies said the laundry room was ransacked, but nothing was stolen.

When Furman found Tiny, the dog was still hot from being spun in the dryer.

* * *

Vladiostok, Russia -- Curiosity got the better of a Russian forester who wanted to know who was living in a big hole in a tree.

He was scared to death, literally, when a large bear jumped out.

The forester suffered a fatal heart attack after the bear leapt from the tree and disappeared into the woods.

Other foresters who discovered their colleague found baby bear cubs living in the hole. However, the foresters decided to leave the cubs alone since the mother was expected to return.

* * *

Washington -- The collapse of a series of beaver dams apparently contributed to a flash flood causing a train derailment that killed five people and seriously injured 26 in Vermont.

Seven cars and both locomotives of the Amtrak "Montrealer" bound from Washington, DC to Montreal derailed.

* * *

New Delhi -- Attracted by the smell of freshly brewed liquor, five thirsty elephants raided a remote tribal village in northeastern India, smashing huts and crushing one man to death.

The elephants tried to get to the vats of the warm brew, but villagers beat drums and ran after the animals with flaming torches.

"The elephants got angry and smashed eight wooden shacks," said a local reporter. One villager was crushed before the elephants returned to nearby forests.

Elephants frequently raid villages in search of liquor and food. India's 20,000 wild elephants are protected by law and cannot be killed until declared rogue.

* * *

Vancouver, British Columbia -- An artist who wants to crush a live rat onto a canvas for art's sake has touched off an angry crusade to save the rat for rat's sake.

The event, planned outside the Vancouver Public Library, enraged animal lovers and prompted several threats against the artist, Rick Gibson.

Gibson planned to snuff Sniffy the rat by placing it between two canvases and drop a 55-pound concrete block on him. His spattered remains would create a "thought-provoking diptych."

* * *

San Juan, Puerto Rico -- Blood-sucking killer leaves trail of dead farm animals throughout the island! Frightened residents wearing fatigues beat bushes in search of mysterious killer!

Whatever it may be, the creature responsible for a string of animal deaths has generated both fear and satire in this U.S. commonwealth.

Goats, hens, rabbits and geese all have fallen prey to the nocturnal killer that reputedly sucks their blood leaving them lifeless. No one can explain why.

Puerto Rico's Dracula had a field night on Halloween with a toll of five goats and 20 parakeets "sucked dead." One newspaper depicted the killer as a pointy-tailed devil.

* * *

Denver -- A squirrel dubbed "Killer T-Rex" for attacking visitors at the city's Museum of Natural History who didn't offer food escaped the death penalty thanks to Governor Roy Romer.

"What did he really do? He bit the hand that fed him." Romer said. "If we start a precedent of punishing people for biting the hand that feeds them, where will that end?"

Visitors said the squirrel would sit on their laps, scratch at their cuffs or grab onto their pant legs in hopes of getting food.

* * *

Johannesburg, South Africa -- A woman on vacation at a game-watching resort was trampled and killed by two hippos as she walked back to her bungalow from a restaurant. Her daughter was seriously injured.

Signs on the path warn guests to avoid hippos, which graze at night alongside the river running through the grounds, but Johanna Nel of Pretoria apparently did not see the animals or hear other people shout warnings.

Hippos are considered among the most dangerous animals in the wild. They charge when people come too close or walk between them and their water supply.

* * *

Brisbane, Australia -- Two crocodiles, believed to be mating, killed a man as his wife and daughter watched from shore. The crocs will be relocated.

Killing the animals would be against the law, said Sgt. Trevor Crawford of Bamaga police in northern Australia.

* * *

Peshawar, Pakistan -- A dispute over a chicken escalated into a pitched battle in which four people were killed, after two Pakistani tribal families tried to settle the row with rocket launchers and hand grenades.

The clash occurred after the bird flew to a nearby house whose owner laid claim to it.

REST IN PEACE

West Palm Beach, FL -- Police planted a bug on a woman's body in her coffin hoping her boyfriend would confess to killing her. But all the listening device on Tracy Lynn Green, 22, picked up was the sound of the boyfriend sobbing.

The boyfriend, Michael Odom, had been charged with killing Ms. Green. Odom, 30, contends Ms. Green jumped to her death from his van as the couple drove along Interstate 95 after a party in Port St. Lucie.

* * *

Morristown, Tenn -- A man who stole a hearse didn't realize there was a body in the back.

"He was walking by and saw the hearse with the motor running and decided he didn't want to walk anymore," a police official said.

The mortuary hearse had transported a body from a nursing home to Humana Hospital, where the body was to be officially pronounced dead. The driver was inside the hospital when the hearse was taken.

* * *

Watertown, CT -- Dennis Sheehey used to say "Boop, Boop Ba Do, I Love You" religiously. But the Catholic Church doesn't think it's an appropriate epitaph for his tombstone.

Now, Sheehey's family is asking the state to intervene. They want to be allowed to engrave "Boop, Boop Ba Do, We Love You" on the grave marker at the Mount Olivet Cemetery in Watertown.

"He always said 'Boop, Boop Ba Do, I Love You," said Sheila Gentile of Plymouth, Sheehey's sister. "He said it to my kids, to all of us. It was him."

Officials at the cemetery, which is run by the Archdiocese of Hartford, rejected an application for the epitaph, saying it did not comply with a policy of only allowing epitaphs that "keep with the Christian tradition."

* * *

Worcester, MA -- Alfred A. Mandella loved his car so much, his family included it in his funeral procession. But the shiny, cream-colored sedan also looked pretty special to a thief.

The 1992 Ford LTD Crown Victoria was stolen while parked outside Our Lady of Mt. Carmel-St. Ann Church during Mandella's funeral mass.

"I can't believe this, for someone to take his car at his funeral," said Mandella's niece. "I guess you have to be very careful, even at your own funeral."

* * *

Cross Plains, Tenn. -- Anxious relatives opened kinfolks' graves after several families discovered that their loved ones had been buried with trash in their coffins or with no coffin at all.

Some families who hired funeral director Bobby Wilks have found bottles, newspapers, discarded flower arrangements and bags of hair in caskets. Some caskets were not protected by vaults that had been paid for.

"One (corpse) had an old metal flower pot on top of his head. It was like he (Wilks) was mad at them all," said gravedigger Darrell Dowdell.

Wilks was charged with six counts of obtaining money under false pretenses.

Wiks would ask family members to leave the graveside before the caskets were lowered into the ground and covered.

"Honey would drip out of his mouth," said one disgruntled customer. "He would come over and put his arm around you and say it would be best if the family didn't see the casket put in the ground and the dirt thrown on top."

At least two caskets were found buried on their sides, and one was left open with an arm hanging out. At least 10 caskets contained trash, and one body was uncovered with no casket at all.

* * *

Sheridan, Wyo. -- Two funeral directors left a casket with a body inside at a Wyoming social services office to protest government reimbursement rates for indigent burials.

P.J. Kane and Mark Ferries, who work with different Sheridan funeral homes, said they meant no disrespect, but just wanted to get the attention of the Department of Public Assistance and Social Services, which sets the limit for indigent burial expenses.

* * *

Pine Bluff, Ark. -- To the dismay of those who loved Nolan Parks III, there's no longer a tombstone marking his grave at Graceland Cemetery.

"I didn't know what happened to it," said his grandmother, Mable Parks.

What happened was that the monument was repossessed by Dunlap's Pine Bluff Monument Co., who said the family still owed $152.

"I never heard of a monument company repossessing a headstone," said Parks' sister, Kathleen Ladd.

Ms. Ladd said she paid $549 for the granite monument and had his picture added for an additional $300. She said she thought she had paid off the bill.

HOME SWEET HOME

Elkhorn City, Ky. -- A 30-ton boulder fell about 500 feet onto a mobile home, crushing a man to death and throwing his grandfather from the couch beside him. The victim's grandmother had just gotten up from the couch.

Jackie Johnson, 19, died when the 10-foot square boulder fell from a cliff behind the house and crashed through the roof onto the sofa where he was sitting.

"When I saw the rock, the only thing I could see was the rock," the victim's grandmother said.

* * *

New York -- A teenager attempting a clandestine meeting with his girlfriend died when the rope he was using to lower himself to her window snapped and he fell 11 stories to his death.

Abdon Ocampo, 18, had tied the rope to a drain pipe on the roof of his girlfriend's apartment building in the Stuyvesant housing complex in lower Manhattan around 1:45 a.m.

He was trying to lower himself one floor to her window when the rope broke.

* * *

Rochester, NY -- A 73-year-old man was found dead in a garbage can on his front porch, where police believe he had been stuck for three days.

Robert Hamm waved to a mailman and a newspaper carrier while in the trash can, but may have been too weak to alert them that he was stuck.

"I would imagine he was probably trying to signal something, but his expression or whatever wasn't enough to get them to do anything about it," Sgt. R. J. Liepins said. "They all feel very bad."

The 11-year-old newspaper carrier, who had waved back to Hamm one day, discovered him dead.

Hamm apparently fell backward into the trash can on his enclosed porch and couldn't get out. He was found in the can up to his armpits, with his legs sticking out.

The mailman saw Hamm in the can from outside the porch and saw his hand move. "He thought something was funny... but he just let it pass," Liepins said.

* * *

New York -- Darren Robinson, a 450-pound rap singer who appeared in two movies during the 1980s as one of the Fat Boys, died after falling off a couch at home.

"I guess when he lost his wind, he went into cardiac arrest," Curtis Robinson said of his 5-foot-11 sibling. "They spent like 45 minutes trying to revive him."

* * *

Chalfont, England -- A frail, 72-year-old woman died after impaling herself on a toilet brush. She was found lying in a pool of blood with her arm draped over the toilet.

Jean Davis apparently tumbled and fell onto the handle of the brush. It went straight through her eye and into her brain.

* * *

Quick Takes

-- A sleeping stripper rolled over in bed and accidentally smothered her husband to death with her 52-inch breasts.

-- After falling sleep while waiting for his waterbed to fill with water, a California man suffocated when the mattress rolled over on him.

-- A man killed his wife when he accidentally drove his car into a freezer in his garage. When the freezer fell, it crushed his wife on the other side of the wall.

-- A 35-year-old Texas man strangled to death when he tripped on a garden hose and got tangled in it.

-- A man awakened by a ringing telephone tried to answer the call, but grabbed a gun from the bedside table instead and accidentally shot himself.

-- An 80-year-old woman pulled down the cupboard bed from the wall of her chalet in Italy and got in. It suddenly snapped closed killing her.

THE FINAL CHAPTER

Chicago -- Family members of a man who was accidentally killed by his own gas have attributed the death to a terrible diet and a room with no ventilation.

When the victim was found, there were no marks on him, but an autopsy showed large amounts of methane gas in his system. His diet had consisted mostly of beans and cabbage.

The man apparently died in his sleep from breathing the poisonous cloud that was hanging over his head. The medical examiner said that if his windows were open, it wouldn't have been fatal, but he was inside an airtight bedroom.

"He was a big man with a huge capacity for creating methane."

Three rescue workers got sick and were hospitalized.

Lake Victoria, Tanzania -- Nine students and a Seventh Day Adventist cleric drowned in what church officials call an accident, but police called stupidity.

On their way to a rally, the ten victims tried to prove their faith by walking on the water. They all drowned in the process.

* * *

Stockholm -- The badly decomposed body of a young man was found sitting on a toilet in a doctor's waiting room where he had been for at least two months.

The body was discovered by the building workers who noted an unpleasant odor coming from the bathroom. The room had been locked for several months as the building was being rehabilitated.

The only clue to his identification was a pair of pliers found in the cubicle with him.

"We don't know who he was," said inspector Jerry Ohlsson. "Maybe he was a junkie."

* * *

Jerusalem -- Talk about trying to reach someone long distance.

Visitors to Upper Nazareth Cemetery who heard a phone ringing from a grave weren't imagining things. The rings came from a mobile cellular phone one of the mourners dropped in the open grave of Rabbi Pinhas

Miller during the funeral service. By the time the loss was discovered, the grave was already covered, and rabbis decided not to dig it up.

* * *

Laconia, NH -- A man died in a courtroom just as a jury was declaring him innocent of sexual assault.

Francis Cavaliere, 40, began breathing heavy as he stood to face the Superior Court jury. He stiffened and fell to the floor. His wife, a nurse, rushed to the defense table where Cavaliere had collapsed.

"There were six verdicts, and as the last one was coming in, he collapsed at that point," said Cavaliere's lawyer.

* * *

Hartford -- Court officials have figured out why Hartford residents were excluded from Federal grand jury pools for three years: The computer that selected names thought everyone in the city was dead.

Federal District Court workers discovered the computer error while investigating why no Hartford residents had been on lists of prospective grand jurors.

The city's name had been listed in the wrong place on computer records, forcing the "d" at the end of "Hartford" into the column used to describe the status of prospective jurors. "D" stands for dead.

So every time the names of Hartford residents popped up for jury duty, the computer noted the deaths and declined to send them juror questionnaires.

* * *

Paris -- One of the more grisly investments imaginable is a bet on when someone will die. Yes, yes, that's what life insurance is all about. But that's abstract death.

Thirty years ago, a French lawyer bet on a specific life, exchanging a $500-a-month annuity for the rights to a 90-year-old woman's apartment when she died. He had paid her more than $185,000 when he died, three times what the apartment is worth.

The woman, Jeanne Calment, is now 121 years old. On birthdays, she always wrote the lawyer, "Sorry I am still alive."

Calment is recognized as the oldest living person.